Five Star Reviews!

Cute book for family night! - "I just got this to add to our family night, a time for the kids to really enjoy handing out with their parents - this is definitely a keeper for those evenings. The jokes are cute & funny - and some are even bit yucky, but boys love that stuff! If you're looking for a family joke book to pass around or add to your game night with the kids - this is it! Lots of funny one liners and laughs here! Cute book!"

Kids Loved It! - "These jokes are perfect for kids. Of course that usually means they're groaners for adults, but even I laughed out loud at many of them. My favorite? "Why can't a Zombie's nose be 12 inches long?" Well...you'll have to read the book to find out"

Zombie

Kids Jokes

Will Work for Brains

By P. T. Hersom

Hersom House Publishing

Ocala, Florida

Zombie Kids Jokes: Will Work for Brains

By P. T. Hersom

© Copyright 2013 P. T. Hersom

First Published, 2013

Printed in the United States of America

Hersom House Publishing

3365 NE 45th St, Suite 101

Ocala, Florida 34479

For Gabriel, who loves to play Hide and Go Seek, Zombie style throughout the house with Mommy and Daddy, ahhh......!

105 Zombie Jokes Plus a Few Extra

10 Zombies

1. Q: Where should a 500 pound Zombie go?

A: On a diet.

2. Q: What did one Zombie say to the other?

A: You look a bit fleshed.

3. Q: Why do Zombies have big fingers?

A: Because they have big boogers.

4. Q: What do you call a Zombie named Lee that no one talks to?

A: Lonely.

5. Q: Why couldn't the Zombie play cards?

A: Because he lost his last hand.

6. Q: Why were the Zombies so tired on April 1st?

A: They had just finished a March of 31 days.

7. Q: Why can't Zombie's nose be 12 inches long?

A: Because then it would be a foot!

8. Q: Why is the Zombie calendar so popular?

A: Because it has a lot of dates!

9. Q: What is it that even the most careful Zombie overlooks?

A: His nose!

10. Q: Why did the Zombie go to bed every night?

A: Because the bed wouldn't come to him!

20 Zombies

11. Q: How does a Zombie say hello?

A: Pleased to eat you.

12. Q: Why did the Zombie go out with a prune?

A: Because he couldn't find a date!

13. Q: Why do Eskimo Zombies do their laundry in Tide?

A: Because it's too cold out-tide!

14. Q: How did the Zombie cure his headache?

A: He put his head through a window and the pane just disappeared!

15. Q: Why did the Zombie run around his bed?

A: To catch up on his sleep!

16. Q: Why did the Zombie take a bath before he robbed the bank?

A: He wanted to make a clean get away!

17. Q: What happened when the Zombie ate the comedian?

A: He felt funny!

18. Q: Why do the Zombies like to eat snails?

A: Because they don't like fast food!

19. Q: What kind of candy do Zombies eat on the playground?

A: Recess pieces.

20. Q: Why did the picture of the Zombie go to jail?

A: Because it was framed.

30 Zombies

21. Q: Why didn't the Zombie starve in a desert?

A: Because of all the sand which is there.

22. Q: In which school did the Zombie learn to make ice cream?

A: Sunday school.

23. Q: Why did the Zombie eat the short man?

A: He was craving short ribs..............OH NOOOOOOO!!

24. Q: What kind of keys do Zombie kids like to carry?

A: Kooo-kies!

25. Q: Why couldn't the zombie cross the road?

A: He was dead tired.

26. Q: Why was there thunder and lightning in the Library?

A: The Zombies were brainstorming!

27. Q: What is the same size and shape of a Zombie, but weighs nothing?

A: His shadow.

28. Q: What should you know if you want to capture a Zombie?

A: More than the Zombie does.

29. Q: Why won't Zombies eat clowns?

A: Because they taste funny.

30. Q: What is a Zombie's favorite sandwich?

A: A Manwich.

40 Zombies

31. Q: What did the Zombie do after he crossed the road?

A: Eat the chicken.

32. Q: Why do Zombies walk silly?

A: Because they can't run, silly!

33. Q: What do you get when you cross a Zombie and a snowman?

A: Frostbite.

34. Q: Where did the one legged Zombie work?

A: I-Hop.

35. Q: What kind of animal is a Zombie's favorite?

A: Any kind he can catch.

36. Q: What is invisible and smells like brains.

A: Zombie farts.

37. Q: Why did the Zombie cross the playground?

A: To get to the other slide.

38. Q: What's black and white, black and white, black and white?

A: A Zombie penguin rolling down a hill!

39. Q: Why did half a Zombie cross the road?

A: To get to his other side!

40. Q: What Zombie can jump higher than a building?

A: Any Zombie, buildings can't jump!

50 Zombies

41. Q: Why did the Zombie spit out the clown?

A: Because he tasted funny!

42. Q: Why don't Zombies like dumb blondes?

A: Because they have no brains.

43. Q: Did you hear the Zombie joke about the roof?

A: Never mind it's over your head.

44. Q: What streets do Zombies live on?

A: Dead ends.

45. Q: Why did the one handed Zombie cross the road?

A: He saw the second hand shop open.

46. Q: Why did the Zombie put sugar on his pillow every night?

A: So he could have sweet dreams.

47. Q: Why did the Zombie go to the bank?

A: Because he was low on moany.

48. Q: What do you call a Zombie that never farts around people?

A: A private tutor.

49. Q: Why did the Zombie wake up exhausted?

A: He dreamt that he was a muffler.

50. Q: What does the Zombie say to his date?

A: It's nice eating you.

60 Zombies

51. Q: Why do Zombies like smart blondes?

A: Because they have brains.

52. Q: Why did the Zombie get fired from the calendar factory?

A: He took a day off.

53. Q: What do you do when a Zombie farts?

A: Get out of the way.

54. Q: Why was the girl afraid of the Zombie?

A: He was all bite and no bark.

55. Q: What is a Zombie's favorite mode of transportation?

A: A blood vessel.

56. Q: How did the Zombies fall in love?

A: It was love at first bite.

57. Q: Why do Zombies scare people?

A: Because they are bored to death.

58. Q: How did the Zombie say good bye to the vampire?

A: So long sucker.

59. Q: Where do Zombies go for a good laugh?

A: The Zomedy Club.

60. Q: What does a Zombie put on top of his ice cream sundae?

A: Whipped scream.

70 Zombies

61. Q: When a Zombie needs a detective who does he call?

A: Sherlock Moans.

62. Q: What kind of makeup do Zombies wear?

A: Mas scare a.

63. Q: What is a Zombie's favorite vegetable?

A: Zom-cchini.

64. Q: Where does the Zombie go to work out?

A: Zomba class.

65. Q: When does a Zombie eat breakfast?

A: In the moaning.

66. Q: What is a Zombie's favorite party game?

A: Hide and Go Eat.

67. Q: When do Zombies cook their brains?

A: On Fry Days.

68. Q: What is a Zombie's favorite rock song?

A: Moany, Moany.

69. Q: Where do Zombies like to swim?

A: In the Dead Sea.

70. Q: What does a Zombie kid call his parents?

A: Zommy and Deady.

80 Zombies

71. Q: Why did the young lady want to go out with the old Zombie?

A: Because she liked him for his moany.

72. Q: What do Zombies say before eating?

A: Zom appetite.

73. Q: Where is the favorite place Zombies love to eat?

A: The body shop.

74. Q: What did the Zombie say to the vampire?

A: You suck.

75. Q: What did the Zombie see at the disco?

A: The Boogie Man.

76. Q: Who won the Zombie beauty contest?

A: Zom-body.

77. Q: What do Zombie kids love to eat?

A: Mac Zombie Nuggets.

78. Q: What do Zombies use in their hair?

A: Scare spray.

79. Q: Why couldn't the Zombie go out with his friends?

A: He didn't have enough moany.

80. Q: What's a Zombie's favorite bean?

A: A human bean.

90 Zombies

81. Q: How did the Zombie pull his muscle?

A: In Zomba class.

82. Q: How do you keep a Zombie from biting his nails?

A: Give him screws.

83. Q: What's a Zombie's favorite dessert?

A: I scream!

84. Q: Do Zombies eat gummy worms with their fingers?

A: No, they eat their fingers separately.

85. Q: How do you make a Zombie dance?

A: Give him a little boogie.

86. Q: Why did the Zombie climb the glass wall?

A: To see what was on the other side.

87. Q: How do you keep a Zombie in suspense?

A: I'll tell you tomorrow.

88. Q: What does a brain + 2 eyeballs =?

A: A good lunch.

89. Q: What does a homeless Zombie's cardboard sign say?

A: Will work for brains.

90. Q: What is a Zombie's favorite breakfast cereal?

A: Brain flakes.

100 Zombies

91. Q: How does a Zombie unclog the kitchen sink?

A: He uses Brain-O.

92. Q: What does a Zombie look like when it's dark?

A: The same as he does in the day time.

93. Q: Why did the Zombie take the toilet to the party?

A: Because he was a party pooper.

94. Q: What did the Zombie order for takeout?

A: Pizza with everyone on it.

95. Q: What kind of music did the one legged Zombie like.

A: Hip Hop.

96. Q: What has six letters and starts with a fart?

A: A Zombie.

97. Q: Which Zombie runs faster, Cold or Hot?

A: Hot, everyone can catch Cold.

98. Q: What happened when the Zombie swallowed a clock?

A: He got ticks.

99. Q: What kind of girl does a Zombie take on a date?

A: Any old girl he can dig up.

100. Q: What comes out at night and goes "Munch, munch, ouch!"

A: A Zombie with a rotten tooth.

105 Zombies

101. Q: What do Zombies call people?

A: Breakfast, lunch and dinner.

102. Q: What's a Zombie's favorite number?

A: Ate.

103. Q: How do you know when a Zombie farted under your bed?

A: When your nose hits the ceiling.

104. Q: What did the Zombie say after he ate the dog?

A: Doggone.

105. Q: What color is a Zombie burp?

A: Burple.

Knock, Knock Zombie

Knock knock...

Who's there?

Zom.

Zom who?

Zombie eatin' you.

Knock knock...

Who's there?

Thumping.

Thumping who?

Thumping green and scary wants to eat your brains.

Can You Read Zombie?

Q: Can you read Zombie?

A: Fi you can raed this whit no porlbem, you aer smrat. Shaer ti whit yuor fienrds.

Bonuses Jokes

Q: What makes more noise than a Zombie?

A: Two Zombies.

Q: How the Zombie cover his bald spot?

A: With a Zomb-over.

Q: Where do Zombies go on their dates?

A: Walmart, they fit right in.

Zombie had a little lamb, little lamb, little lamb,

Zombie had a little lamb...

Mooaannn... "Gulp" Not anymore!

More Zombie Fun

Would you like to add some hilarious "Zombie Approved" fun to your child's birthday party? Then check out P. T. Hersom's "Zombie Party Ideas for Kids: How to Party Like a Zombie". Be prepared, a mob of Zombies are ready to invade your home and stir up some kid friendly fun. Get it now on Amazon Kindle or paperback!

Zombie Party Ideas for Kids: How to Party Like a Zombie

Enjoyed the Book?

Thank You for Buying This Book. I was hoping you could help your fellow book enthusiast out. When you have a free second, please leave your honest feedback about this book on Amazon. I certainly want to thank you in advance for doing this.

To see new releases by P. T. Hersom and many other fun things for kids, go to:

www.Pthersom.com

Other Books to Enjoy by P. T. Hersom

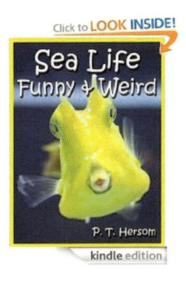

Sea Life Funny & Weird Marine Animals

Made in the USA
Lexington, KY
16 July 2014